WHO IS SHE

Inspirational Stories for Women

DARA LY

Copyright © 2024 Dara Ly
All Rights Reserved.

This book is licensed for your personal enjoyment only. It may not be resold or given away to other people without prior agreement from the author. If you would like to share this book with another person, please purchase an additional copy for each recipient. If you're reading this book and did not purchase it, or it was not purchased for your use only, please kindly purchase your own copy. Thhank you for respecting the work of the author.

Table of Contents

Introduction 1

Part 1: Her Personal Issues 2

Part 2: Her Relationship Issues 26

Part 3: Her Personal Rules 47

Part 4: Because She Can 69

Dedicated to DARA LY Books Fans!

Legal Notice

The author has strived to be as accurate and complete as possible in the creation of this book, notwithstanding the fact that he does not warrant or represent at any time that the contents within are perfectly accurate due to the rapidly changing nature of information transformation.

Although all attempts have been made to verify information provided in this book, the author assumes no responsibility for errors, omissions, or contrary interpretation of the subject matter herein.

Any perceived slights of specific persons, people, or organizations are unintentional.

In practical advice books, like anything else in life, there are no guarantees. Thus, readers are cautioned to rely on their own judgment about their individual circumstances to act accordingly.

This book is not intended for use as a source of professional advice. The readers are advised to seek services of competent professionals in the fields.

Acknowledgements

First of all, I'd like to thank my editor Sovanchanbomey Chith. With your great patience in editing, this book is made possible. We made it, at last. Thank God!

I also want to thank my illustrator Champey Ouk for a beautiful book cover design. I also want to thank Sophorn Phorn for allowing me to use your photo for this book cover. It's beautiful.

I want to thank Dyna Sao, Somonyroth Rin, and Nita Sim for proofreading this book. Thank you for your help.

I want to thank fans of DARA LY Books for telling such great stories. You own a big part of this book. You know who you are.

Last but not least, I'd like to thank *D2D Print* for publishing this book. Thhank you for your great service.

About the Author

DARA LY is the graduate from the University of Puthisastra (UP), bachelor degree of English Literature. He's the Chairman of DARA LY Books, a small book publishing group serving the readers on the topics, such as education, inspiration, and entertainment.

As a lifelong reader, he has founded **DARA LY Reading Space** to open the study clubs for the young generation of Cambodia. He is determined to keep his clubs free of charge, as always.

Since September 5, 2016, Dara Ly has published 15 books, all are for teenagers in Cambodia. His goal is simple (and he's silly enough to pursue it). He wants to encourage young Cambodian people to read 50 books a year.

Introduction

The book "**Who Is She**" tells the stories of the lives of many young women who are the winners but still get lost or confused between the world around them and their own world. There are 4 parts which illustrate 40 lessons about 40 unique characters in this book. Notably, you will read and learn about the problems and solutions provided in each lesson. In addition to the third person pronoun "she" being used in each lesson, you will get to meet another main character known as the Machine who speaks to inspire you, encourages you to believe in yourself, and gives you some suggestions to deal with your problems.

Part 1 will remind you more about the problems that happen to you personally. You may be able to find some suggestions too.

Part 2 will review the problems that you consider relationship issues, including friendship and family. You can find some motivating messages in that part too.

Part 3 will show you how women handle everything, in good times and bad. Some lessons are remarkably inspiring. You will learn something from that part.

Part 4 will give you some ideas about how to define your own life the ways you want. There are ten different ways, to be exact. I hope you like each one of them.

Good luck, **My Reader!**

DARA LY

Part 1
HER PERSONAL ISSUES
Motivation from Machine!

WHO IS SHE

1
Failure
She Failed the Exam

Who is she?

She thinks she is a loser because she failed the exam. It came as a surprise, and she was quite shocked to learn that she failed. Tears were rolling down her cheeks. She ran to her mom and hugged her. She needed motivation as she also felt ashamed of herself, not knowing what to say. She just kept crying and crying.

It's unexpected to fail, but it's obvious that she has to make a new plan for her future. It's the future that seems pretty lonely. Her friends will go on to study at universities, but she will be stuck at the same high school. In other words, she has to repeat the 12th grade again, unwillingly and shamefully.

She hates being compared by others, but sometimes she compares herself with her friends and classmates. As a result, she gets mad at herself. When she looks in the mirror, she sees a loser, and she just wants to...

Motivation from Machine

Hello. My name is **Dara Ly the Machine**, but you can call me **Cool Mac**. My Creator (**Dara Ly the Human**) has invented me to speak on behalf of him, so my job is to talk with you. You can talk back if you want.

You feel ashamed because you think failing an exam is a bad thing. What do you want me to say? Do you need an answer or an honest answer?

A good answer would be: Don't think too much. An honest answer would be: Think and ask!

You heard me. Ask people. Think about what they have to say. By the way, make sure you ask the right things to the right people. However, do not believe them 100% because nobody can have all the answers you need. Failing an exam is only scary before you fail. After failing it, you don't feel scared anymore. *Are you willing to change the way you think about the exam?*

Time! Brain! Feelings!

Do you have time? Yes. Your priority right now is to pass that exam.

Are you smart? Yes. You can be smart.

Can you control your feelings? Yes. You can work well when you feel good.

WHO IS SHE

2
Comparison
She Hates It

Who is she?

She is just a girl with a simple wish. Her wish is to be happy. People around her, however, don't want that to happen. They just want to upset her because they like to compare. They don't know that they're killing her emotionally when they're comparing like that. She hates being compared, and she hates it when they keep doing that. They keep telling her that she is no good. What is her response? Her response is silence.

There are two forms of silence. The first one is the silence with confidence. The second one is the silence with pain. Her silence has sent a clear message about her pain. Sadly, nobody can hear nor see it. Nobody sees her pain, and nobody cares about her feelings.

There are hundreds of stories that she wants people to know, yet she can't speak out. Why? Because she's busy crying. As a matter of fact, she's crying right now.

(I hate it when I have to remind her about those dramatic and sad things that she has to go through, again.)

Sometimes she becomes convinced that she is just a loser, and some people just don't stop comparing. They keep comparing her with other kids. She is convinced that something is wrong with her, and...

Motivation from Machine

You are upset because people keep comparing you with others. What do you want me to say? What? Do you need motivation? You want me to say something nice or something brutally honest?

You think that those kids are better than you, so you must be a loser. If I have to be honest with you, I would say that it is the most laughable thing I've ever heard. Well, let me try to be a little nicer. Okay? I would say that you are unique in your own way.

I know. I know. Some old farts think that you are just as dumb as they believe you are. The saddest part is that you believe it too. You agree with them, sometimes.

And that, in my Machine opinion, is wrong. It is wrong because those people don't live your life. You do. They don't know you like you know yourself. They don't even care about you, so you shouldn't care about them.

My suggestion: **Walk away!**

When I sense that someone is talking nonsense in front of me, I walk away. Actually, I walk as fast as I run away from fart. They might think that you are arrogant when you walk away from them. If you stay and listen to them, they will compare. Either way, you're no good, in their eyes.

I don't mind when some people think that I'm an arrogant person. They can think or say whatever they want because I don't care what they think. In your heart, you know if you are arrogant or not, right? Self-respect is important. Respect

WHO IS SHE

yourself, and respect others, but do not let anyone disrespect you. Show them that you mean business.

When people are talking nonsense in front of you, you can make the decision. Ignore their words, or let their words ruin your peace of mind!

You choose because you're the boss. Be a smart boss!

3
No Comparison
The Story

Who is she?

She's a little girl who is beautiful and purely good. Sadly, that's not the story she was told when she was younger. Instead, people kept saying that she's ugly and unattractive. Even worse, some people said to her that she was not smart enough. That's a painful experience for a little girl.

As painful as it might sound, it actually changed her life, the hard way. Because of this pain, she decided to be better. Better looking and better mind! But most importantly, she cared more about her study, and she told herself that she wouldn't let anybody else tell her that she's dumb. She tried studying every day. She spent more hours each day doing exercises and reviewing lessons. Her study performance was improved. It sounds very simple, but it's a true story, and it's been successfully tested. If anybody wants to improve study performance, they just need to spend more hours learning. She's proof of this method. She became a better student, and nobody dared to bully her anymore.

Nevertheless, her beauty is also a priority, and indeed, it's an important part of her happiness too. She believes that she can change her image and become more beautiful. She started caring more about her body, her skin, and her healthy diet. No fast food! Okay, sometimes still can't say NO, but she avoids eating too much of it.

But who is she?

She used to suffer, and she wants to tell other girls to be positive and stay strong. Why? Because, as a kid, she used to

WHO IS SHE

be hurt by the words from people around her. She doesn't blame them now. She doesn't blame anybody. She believes that people have different views, and she can have a different idea of how to be happy. This is why she doesn't compare herself with anybody. There is one exception, though. She can compare herself with her old self. She aims at being better than her old version.

But who is this girl?

She has a few quotes for herself and other women:

- *Love yourself before you want others to accept you.*
- *Believe in yourself and help yourself before expecting others to do so.*
- *Do not compare yourself with others.*
- *Do not sleep with your eyes open. (Okay, she didn't say that.)*

4
Her Experiences
She Also Cares about Her Friends

Who is she?

She's a nice woman, but she doesn't like a guy who pretends to be nice only to flirt with her. And her friends also! What she doesn't know is that a guy has a different way of thinking.

Everybody loves an outstanding student, and the outstanding student is good in so many ways, except for one. He likes flirting with so many girls that everyone stops trusting him. Like most girls, she starts to question his intention every time he says something nice. That doesn't mean she dislikes the guy. It's just a tendency to be cautious.

But who is she?

She's a good student, but she just doesn't feel that way. Sometimes she blames herself for not trying hard enough. Often, she worries about the future ahead. One year from now, she's going to take the exam that will define her future. It's a pretty scary thing when she thinks about it because people around her place high expectations on her. That's her life as a grade-12 student!

Expectation motivates her to try hard, but too much of it can also give her a hard time. In other words, she needs to try to be better than she could ever be.

Who is she?

She wants to improve her learning habits. She tries finding something to motivate herself, but she never finds anything good enough to keep her going. As a result, she just goes with the flow, hoping she could go as fast as other students could. That's how she feels each day about studying.

WHO IS SHE

Meanwhile, she also cares about her friends. She wants them to study more, and pass the exam. However, she believes that it's hard to convince them. They think they're dumb, but she thinks they could improve themselves if they only hang out less often and study a little bit more every day.

Who is this grade-12 girl?

5
The Impact
Getting Lost

Who is she?

Comparison is what people like to do, and they do it all the time. One problem, though. They do not know the negative impact it could have on the one being compared. It's a sad thing, but it's hard to avoid. As easy as it might sound, people compare others with many things and anything.

When you are in the middle of this situation, it's kind of annoying. Especially, when it is your family and loved ones who actually bring you to this unwanted happenstance. It's unpleasant, but it's unavoidable.

You might regret the fact that you didn't spend enough time to listen to your heart when you should have. You might feel that it's an unlucky part of your life when other people compare you with someone else.

It's even more upsetting when they keep asking you about the result. Often you get lost, and become stressful with yourself and your life too. That's the sad part, but that's not the whole picture. Believe me, that's only the beginning.

The suggestion is: **Appreciate what you can do now rather than trying to answer all kinds of questions.**

You've been taught to believe in reason and reject something outside of your comfort zone. That's what limits your mind from greatness. Your creativeness can't function properly if you limit your imagination. I'm not saying that we should block our reasoning.

We should balance between reason and faith. We should accept both logic and magic. People compare because they're

WHO IS SHE

scared. Their logic makes them scared. You should be worried no more, for the magic is in your mind. Free your mind from the burden of having to please everybody. Believe me, not everyone wants to hurt you, but sometimes good intentions can hurt you, more than they could imagine.

6
What About It?
Bully

Who is she?

She: Author, can I share about the topic bully?
Me: Yeah, sure. What about it?
She: My friends bully me. They say that I'm too cute.
Me: Wait, what?
She: Yeah.
Me: Okay, next book title, "*Proud to Be Cute.*"
She: Huh?

You Are Perfect in Your Own Way

Who are you?

I can tell you that you are great, and you are perfect in your own way. You don't need to do a lot of makeup stuff to make yourself look beautiful because your beauty speaks for itself.

You would say, "*Oh, come on, this author doesn't know what he's talking about.*"

Maybe I don't, or maybe I do.

Let me repeat, "*You are great and perfect in your own way.*"

You can transform yourself into a mature woman. Your greatness is your true beauty. Be yourself and do everything in a great way. What way? A way followed by your heart!

Some Quotes

- *Mistakes can make you wiser.*
- *Your life is your freedom, not an obligation.*
- *Your life is about your greatness and creativeness, not your failure.*
- *Your life is about you, not others.*
- *If you want an independent lifestyle, you should focus on what you love to do.*
- *You don't need to worry too much about other people and what they have to say about you.*
- *Believing is seeing.*
- *If you believe you are weak, you'll see many weak points in yourself.*
- *If you believe you are strong, you'll see many strong points in yourself.*
- *If you believe you are beautiful, you'll know how to use editing apps.*

(Wait, what?)

WHO IS SHE

7

Her Disappointment
She Has Never Heard Anything Nice

Who is she?

She's a good student, and a clever kid, but she never knows how to stay away from disappointment. The thing is, she is always disappointed with herself for not being able to perform better so that her parents could be proud of her. Nevertheless, her study result has always been phenomenal, yet she has never heard anything nice or encouraging from her parents. That's what makes her upset from time to time. She just wishes they would say something good, but that's a wish that would perish.

She would rather keep everything to herself than to discuss with anybody at home even though she knows it might have been better to let her mom know what's on her mind or what she wants. It pains her to hide the truth from the people she loves, but it's not as painful as to get rejected without explanation.

Who is this girl?

This girl is no dimwit like most people think, but her lack of will to show them is the main obstacle. She has never thought that a little girl like her could one day choose her own way to live her own life. Never once has she dared to question anything being placed onto her shoulders. Will this determine her life forever?

Only she can answer that. Only she can free herself and live her life better. In order for her to do that, she needs education and a proper way of thinking.

Self-education should be a good option for her to reinvent her life the way she wants. Positive thinking with a reality check could also be good for her, shall this girl become more mature. Last but not least, she has to have a strong will to get what she wants. Otherwise, she would remain unhappy and disappointed.

This counterargument is not groundless, for she has repeatedly blamed herself for not reaching the highest level that people expect from her. That's a hard way every smart person has to overcome. She is no exception, so to speak.

If she wants to become stronger, she needs to get rid of the helplessness mentality. In other words, her mental strength is as strong as a wind in December, but the way she views her mental attitude couldn't be any worse. She thinks she's helpless, in many ways. She never believes that she could ever fulfill the expectation of her parents. She's the first child, and it is only fair to expect more from her. That's what she thinks. She also fears that she would let her family down if she cannot do well in study.

But who is this helpless girl?

Helplessness is not the right word to define this girl, according to her friends and people who know her well. Her boyfriend, for example. You can ask him whether or not she's a smart girl. Believe me, he would say yes. I mean, who wouldn't? Her study record is also the evidence to prove that she's an outstanding student and a clever girl. Her IELTS test score is 7.5, and that's considered high, given the fact that it's not her native language test.

Even though she's a super star among her peers, it is not enough to be validated or acknowledged by her parents.

Sometimes what she needs to hear is: "*You're great. You've done the best.*"

WHO IS SHE

Suggestion from Machine: **It's only one side of the coin. The best is yet to come. You'll see.**

8
Hard Work
Her Belief

Who is she?

She believes in hard work, learning, perfecting her skills, and becoming useful. These are the elements that make her successful, and busy each day. She likes to be busy with what she loves to do. She loves her job, and she wants to take it to the next level.

Self-education is important to her. The power of education is so powerful it can transform a person. It can lift her out of poverty also.

If you want to measure your success, you should write it down. Ignore the outside noises; they are not important. You need to focus on your goal, and work each day to get closer to the measurement of success. Look deep down, inside yourself, and you'll know whether you're moving up or going down. Always be cautious about what you choose to do each day. What you do will make or break you. It's the habit we're talking about here. If you keep getting better and better at maintaining a good habit, soon enough it will become your second nature. You'll be able to do what you do best, and it will look effortless.

Please keep that in mind.

9
A Scholarship Program
Her Dream & Her Family

Who is she?

She's an intelligent person, but she always doubts herself and her ability. She's never thought she's good enough to apply for a scholarship. Despite that, she didn't give up on her dream to study abroad. She applied for a scholarship program and got selected to the final round. That's another level, she thought. She was excited for the result until the selection committee sent the financial assessment form to her family to fill. The form required information about the family incomes.

Since she lives with her aunt, that is a much bigger challenge, provided that the additional expenses, such as flight ticket and pocket money would have to be sponsored by her aunt. She did not share the same excitement with her niece when she found out that the expenses were a lot, and beyond her ability to provide. Her concern was not without ground, however.

Getting a scholarship might sound like a fantastic dream for the young girl, but the reality of the family financial situation does not allow this dream to take place just yet. Everybody was happy but upset at the same time.

One night her aunt said to her: "*You should limit your dream. Stop dreaming of studying abroad at this age because you're too young for that. Your father is getting old and without a high income. He can't afford that although he very much wants to.*"

Who is she?

DARA LY

Her father rarely talks to her, and she feels the same way, but it's not uncommon. She calls him only when she seriously needs the money for study. Does she love her father? No doubt about that. Does he love her? He does, but in a way that she could never comprehend. Is their relationship good? It depends on who answers.

The scholarship opportunity didn't come very often, and this time, she was hoping to be selected. Be that as it may, she understood that her biggest obstacle was her family finance. Understandably, she could not ask from her aunt, and she did not expect anything encouraging from her father either.

He's a tough man, and he's not the kind of sweet-talk daddy. She thought that he would rip apart the remaining pieces of dream for scholarship (if her aunt hadn't done the job yet). She thought wrong!

Her father said: *"If your aunt cannot help us, well, I'll try as much as I can. I'm going to sell our land. It's worth $9,000 or a little less, but it'll do."*

It's a big gamble for the family, so to speak. If she passed the scholarship, that would mean the family had to sell the land to support her, given the fact that it was not fully-funded.

She had to go through the interviewing, which was the final round. She thought that she would fail, because she didn't answer well. After 2 months, the result was out, and she did fail. She cried so hard she couldn't eat for days. She had invested so much in this opportunity, and it flew away just like a bird. This experience had taught her a few things, however. She might not be able to study abroad just yet, but she did learn another aspect of her family. Yeah!

WHO IS SHE

Why try to learn about other people from other countries when you should learn and understand your family a little bit more? Right? I don't know. You tell me!

She's learned a few things about herself and her family:

- *Never doubt yourself.*
- *In hard times, you'll know who's on your side.*
- *Appreciate what your family is doing for you, still.*
- *You need to keep fighting for your dream.*
- *Failure is a mean teacher, but you can do better if you can learn from this sucker. I mean, failure!*

10
Her Dream
To Become an Author

Who is she?

Publishing a book could be difficult, but writing it could be a painstakingly tremendous challenge for a junior student. Let alone the self-development book that she really wants to write about.

This is the story of a girl who wants to tell the world that a girl is capable of doing many things if she focuses on her strength. She has spent many late nights writing and rewriting until she could get it right. It's a grueling process, so to speak, but she is willing to work hard to tell her stories in her first book.

Now she's half-way to get her book published, and I'm working with her to make it happen.

If you want to become an author, here are the 5 steps you may need to know:

Step 1: Writing

Step 2: Editing

Step 3: Publishing

Step 4: Branding

Step 5: Sales & Marketing.

If you want to become an author and want to learn more details about these 5 steps, please talk to me directly through my Facebook page: DARA LY Books.

You know I have the experiences that can assist you with the writing and the money to help you with the publishing, right? But most importantly, I am a full-time promoter of reading culture in Cambodia. I want to see Cambodian people

WHO IS SHE

reading many great books by our great authors who have listened, talked and learned from real people with real problems. I am more than happy to help you if you want to become an author.

Meanwhile, I also want you to be mentally prepared before choosing to do this work. I want you to know some strange habits that most authors have.

Author usually works alone in a small room. You are not going out often because you are busy reading and

writing every second you are awake. If you're not reading or writing, you would be spending time thinking and learning about things in your head.

Author has a strange sleeping habit. Author often forgets to eat.

Some authors have some strange personalities.

Author doesn't care much about his appearance at times.

Author loves to read.

Author loves to watch movies.

Author loves to hear feedback from his readers.

The list can go on!

DARA LY

Part 2
Her Relationship Issues
Some Stories!

WHO IS SHE

11
Her Parents
She Wants Freedom

Who is she?

She is just a daughter loved and protected by her parents, yet she is not very happy about her life because something is missing. Actually, she wants freedom to live her life, but she is faced with rejection time and time again. The fact of the matter is that her parents are not ready to grant her total freedom yet.

Parents are the protectors. It's a good thing to have protective parents. You'll never know what's ahead of you. You'll never understand the concept of parenthood until you become a parent.

One thing that all parents know is that they too used to be children. Thus, parents should at least permit their children to do what's right for them, instead of keeping them under strict control. They should let their children grow by themselves.

She cannot blame her parents. She cannot blame herself as well, but she doesn't know what to do. To obey her parent's orders or to be an independent person?

Truth be told that she wants to be alone, but her parents wouldn't let her. They have good reason for keeping her, given the fact that she's still young, in their eyes. Sometimes it's hard to reject her parents' advice, but she knows it's even harder to accept it.

When you're in the middle of the options and unable to decide by yourself, all you can do is to skip the problem and let the problem be the problem without a solution.

Sometimes she agrees with her parents about the decisions she can make. Sometimes she disagrees. Either way, she has to compromise every time the conversation involves her parents. Nevertheless, it's a good thing that she could talk openly with them. Some parents are not that open-minded about what their children can or can't do.

Who is she?

She doesn't express her views that much, but her face could often speak her mind and let her mom know that she doesn't want to follow the advice. At an early age, she wouldn't show any sign of disagreement with her parents, but that changes when she grows up. Her mom could see that, but she's not ready to let her daughter fly solo in the jungle. It is debatable whether her mother is right to keep the daughter protected at all times. Undoubtedly, she is right about one thing; the place outside home is not always safe for a girl. There are bad people everywhere, and bad things could happen to her daughter too, she fears. Every parent feels the same way about this, and they can't be blamed for being a protective parent.

How protective should they be?

Let's put it this way: How much freedom should a daughter be given by the parents?

How responsible should a daughter be if she wants independence to live her life?

Suggestion from Machine

Suggestion from Machine: **You decide!**

Trust your instinct, and follow your heart, but make sure nobody follows you on the road while you're riding a motorbike. To avoid that, you have to be smart and always careful. It won't hurt to remain careful and well- calculated.

WHO IS SHE

It'll help you grow stronger and more confident in your own decision. If you can prove to your parents that you're a thoughtful person, they'll surely give you all the freedom you need. All parents love their children, but every parent needs assurance that every child is safe and safe. Nothing but safe!

Keep in mind that if you want independence, you need to be responsible for your decision. You could be wrong sometimes, but that's okay. Everybody makes a few mistakes from time to time, but make sure you can fix the errors of your actions. If you can do that, then your parents would let you rule your own life. Believe me, been there, done that!

There's one lesson I've learned about my parents. They were not always supportive of my decision about my life. Almost every decision I made was questioned or even rejected by my mother, and, to be fair, my father rarely said anything about anything. As a young person, I thought that I was against everyone at home. To be honest, I thought that the whole world was against me! It's a miserable way to live my life, I can tell you that.

It took me nearly ten years to realize that both of them only want the best for me. Now my idea about my parents has changed dramatically, and I start to reverse my thoughts about myself and my family. Instead of opposing all the ideas from my parents, I propose a strong partnership with them. Now they listen to me, and they appreciate my ideas also. Instead of trying to win over their argument, I propose a win-win solution. I know, I wouldn't have believed me too if I had said this to myself five years ago. This is why my only suggestion for you is: **You decide!**

12
Friends
Friendship

Who is she?

She is a good person, and she surrounds herself with many good friends. However, some friends are not good, and oftentimes they bring her problems. Even worse, they break her trust. Trust issues have become her main concern about friendship. She decides to hide herself from some friends because she is fed up with the same problems that keep coming. She never wants to end her friendship, but the hardship brought by some friends never seems to end. She has no choice but to finish it before it finishes her.

Maybe she expects too much from her friends? Maybe she just believes those promises too much? Maybe she is naïve enough to think that nothing has changed when everything is changing continuously? Maybe she is too loyal?

After this lesson, she has changed and become more careful. Never again would she let people come into her life easily. She would be more careful before she could trust anyone again.

Sometimes mistakes can be made, but oftentimes people couldn't forgive nor forget. It comes to a point where expectation does hurt, and friendship does fall apart. People who are nice to others can also feel disappointed.

Suggestion from Machine

Suggestion from Machine: **You can select a few good friends.**

WHO IS SHE

I have had a few good friends for more than ten years, and our friendship is as healthy as a bull. I mean, it's strong and unbreakable because it has been tested many times over the years. Be that as it may, it didn't get smooth all the time. There were times when I also had trust issues and didn't want to share my secrets with my friends. I thought they might turn these secrets against me someday. I was wrong; they never did because we respected each other.

Another issue among my peers was jealousy. We were sort of jealous of one another. I admitted that to

my friends, and they revealed the same feelings about me. They thought that I was more handsome and more attractive. Okay, they didn't say that. I was joking!

But jealousy among friends was real. Back then, I couldn't bear the fact that my friends were doing better than me, and I tried not to talk about that with them. They didn't know what else to talk about rather than to brag about their trips to this country and that country.

Should I be jealous of the fact that they could travel to many places? No, I shouldn't be. In fact, I couldn't care less. Anyway, I couldn't say the same thing about other friends since they were not really happy to know that they're stuck in one place while the other ones were traveling places and meeting new people.

Marriage was another thing that didn't sit well among us, given the fact that we changed girlfriends faster than our clothes. This year alone, three of us got married, and two got engaged while the rest were either single or too broke to get married. To be honest, we are not jealous of the fact that our friends could get married, but the idea that some of us still couldn't find even a girlfriend is pathetic.

This year also taught us a big lesson, and it touches us personally. We've lost one good friend recently. He had gone back to meet the Maker, and may his soul rest in peace.

To me, it touches my soul, and I still grieve for the loss of my good friend because it was unexpected. He should have stayed much longer, but fate had taken him away to a place we cannot reach. YET!

I'm sure none of us (my friends and I) will be jealous of him for leaving us too soon. The lesson here is that we should never be jealous or feel upset when our friends are doing great. Instead, we should be happy for them and hope for the best for them. You don't need to lose a friend just to learn how important it is to have one.

In conclusion, friendship is important, so choose a few friends who could share happiness with you for the rest of your life. Be grateful that they have chosen you to be their friend. Be loyal to them. Be a good friend!

WHO IS SHE

13
Studying
Pressure

Who is she?

She is an outstanding student trying to make her parents proud but only to realize that she's got more and more pressure. At one point, she pauses and asks herself: "Why am I doing what I am doing right now?"

To seek betterment from herself is always great, but to be drowned in the river mud of burden is a disaster. Everyone wants to be an outstanding student, but no one knows how an outstanding student feels when the burden has outsmarted her.

She always has a sense of chaos because she needs to fulfill her dad's wish. She has to make sure she won't let him down because her sisters' achievements are just too great to be compromised with. Wants it or not, she has to do what she is told to do. Of course, everybody would admire her because she has done phenomenal things for herself and for her family. However, nobody would see the pain, regret, disappointment, and the stress that she hides. It's been a long while.

Sometimes she just wants to throw her life away for a little while and takes it back later. She enjoys freedom of choice for a short period of time. At least, she doesn't need to be scared by the unseen future that perhaps never exists in reality.

If it's up to her, she'd rather be a normal student than an outstanding one. It's just an idea that can't be allowed by her father. She has to put her personal preference aside in order to make her parents proud and happy. Her relationship with studying is a love-hate relationship. She loves it because she loves studying. She hates it because she has to study in order to fulfill her parent's wishes. It's like an arranged marriage.

Suggestion from Machine

Suggestion from Machine: **You can study by yourself and for yourself.**

Let's not worry about who says what. Your life is your choice. Your study is no exception. Meanwhile, it is a good thing to be a good student. Agree? Just because you don't want to follow all the ideas from your parents, that doesn't mean you have to throw away your good learning habits, right?

You're a smart person, so you'll get the best result from anything you learn, with or without your parents' forcing. That's the fact, so you don't have to hate what you love. Okay? You don't need to put unnecessary pressure on yourself. Believe me, your parents want the best for you. Maybe they don't try to explain to you why they push you harder than you want, but they mean well. No parent wants his or her child to fail. Certainly, all parents want to see their children grow to be smart and great.

It's not the problem of why they want you to try hard. It's the problem of how. Their way of getting to the top might not be the same as yours, so their pace might somehow seem too fast and too much.

The suggestion is simple. You can reset your own learning pace, and follow your plan. Simple enough?

WHO IS SHE

14
Her Wish
Divorce

Who is she?

She is a little girl loved and raised by a grandmother after her parent's divorce. The divorce of the parents is a painful thing for a child. She is that child, helpless and lonely.

She wishes that she could have traveled back in time to visit her parents. She would have asked them to love each other forever so that their unborn kid (she) could enjoy the richness of love and care from parents. That's her wish. A wish that never comes true! Never will!

She is tired of misery. Other kids have parents when she does not have anyone to rely on. Other kids could cry freely, and the parents would come and check if they are doing okay. When she cries, she just cries from the inside. Nobody knows that, and nobody seems to care.

She does not blame her parents. She does not blame anybody. She only hopes that other children won't have to deal with the same painful experience. It's a lonely feeling.

Anyway, this lonely girl is not alone. She thinks she is alone, but she has one person with her right now. That person is herself. Being alone does not mean a lonely life. Loneliness is just a state of mind. It could be good or bad.

Reminding from Machine

"Being alone sometimes could mean you're stronger and more resilient. You can choose to be unhappy because you're alone, or you can choose to be happy and grateful. I know, it sounds dumb, but God has sent me to remind you that you're never alone. You have yourself. Have faith in yourself!"

WHO IS SHE

15
Being Different
A Strange Girl

Who is she?

She is a strange girl with a strange habit, but in her mind, she knows what she is doing. This person is no ordinary girl, but she has chosen to follow an ordinary path. She chooses to be common just to avoid trouble. She knows her talent is far more powerful than this, but she is not confident enough to challenge herself and get what she deserves. She has chosen the safe road, and she avoids criticism from other people.

Indeed, she deserves to be treated better. Instead, she is criticized so badly by those who do not understand the beauty of being different. Following the reaction of other people, she decides to fake herself, by becoming like the rest. She tries to blend in even though she knows it's uncomfortable.

To her, it isn't strange to be a strange girl, but it will be uncommon if she chooses to be common like the rest. A lot of people would say that this girl is weird, but they don't know that she wants to express herself in her own way. They want her to fit in while she knows that she's unique. They want to tell her what to do, but she knows better what she likes.

The question is: **Should she fit in or stand out?**

16
After High School
University

Who is she?

She has just finished high school, and she wants to pursue higher education in the city. The only problem is that she doesn't know what she could do. University seems new to her, and she has no idea what to do in order to get into one. After high school, there are some obstacles that she is facing.

She doesn't know what to study or what she can do after graduation. She doesn't know much about any jobs and can't ask anybody. She could only rely on her relatives who could help her find a good major. She might have to choose the suggested major even if she doesn't have a clear idea of what to expect from it.

Her English is not good, and she is not confident in using it. She is told that English is crucial for university students. It will put her in a disadvantageous position.

She is afraid of speaking in public, and she is told that she has to speak in front of her classmates soon. This idea has scared her already.

Similarly, communication is her obstacle too since she is a shy person. She doesn't dare to talk to anybody. The fact of the matter is she needs help. She wants to improve her communication, and she wants to build her confidence also. How?

Suggestion from Machine
Suggestion from Machine: **Find the right information!**

WHO IS SHE

Being able to pursue higher education is one thing, but to exceed higher expectations is way too high. By the way, human beings are capable of doing anything. Girl is no stranger to greatness, but she needs to know how to chase it. Education is the key to greatness.

You ask, "But what is the key to education?"

One of the keys to good education is information. Why is information so important? Information changes the situation, and, in fact, it can change your life forever.

If you want to improve your English, you should learn more. Sounds simple? It does sound simple, but many people find it too simple. However, they do not follow this simple plan, and then they start to question it. You don't want to be like a lot of people, right?

The suggestion is: **Read one English book every week.**

What about communication and confidence? How to gain more confidence in communication or public speaking?

The suggestion is: **Read a lot of books and talk to a lot of people.**

Moreover, you should join a public speaking club or any places where people learn and practice public speaking skills. As a freshman, I joined the debate club for two terms. I was still involved in the same club for, at least, two more years.

In short, you should focus on improving yourself. There will be more things you can learn. Have a positive mental attitude, and never allow any obstacles to stop you from achieving your goal. Can you do that? Yes, you can.

17
Her Mind
Opportunity and Responsibility

Who is she?

In the eyes of her parents, she is still a little girl. In her mind, she knows she has grown to be a woman because she wants her own freedom, and she is ready and able to do great things for herself. Being obedient is one thing, but being independent is another thing.

If you think you're the only one facing this issue, then let me reassure you that many people also face the same problem. The problem alone doesn't complete the journey in your life, so you need to find the solution.

She who believes in herself will do the things that nobody believes would be possible. She can listen to her parents, but she can follow her heart also. She knows what she wants. She can take the opportunity to live her life by herself, but she has to be responsible for her own decision. Responsibility is the requirement if she wants to be independent and have freedom.

Who is she?

WHO IS SHE

18
A Strong Girl
Now

Who is she?

A strong girl is a woman that will never let the man control her life once more. Maybe she used to let him get total access to her future plan. Maybe she used to let him know that she was weak. Maybe she used to let him come and stay in her life for a while. Yes, maybe. And, yeah, she used to feel like a dependent girl. She used to believe that her life wouldn't be complete without a man whom she loved.

What about now?

Now? Well, she just changes a little bit. Just a bit. Changing from "used to" to "uses." She uses different types of thoughts. She is strong enough to live alone, meaning that she no longer needs anybody to design a future for her.

You ask, "*What about him?*"

He? Who is he? Does he matter?

She once said, "*But the memory does matter.*" And now, what does she say?

Now she says, "*I want to be a stronger version of myself. I want to be me. To be the brand-new me!*"

She has made up her mind to live alone for a while. Never again would she allow the same drama to ruin her life. Not again! Never again would she let anyone treat her unfairly. Never ever!

Now what she wants is: "*To live as a strong girl with a wise woman mindset.*"

Who is she?

DARA LY

Can it be you? Any woman is great, and every great girl is a wise woman.

19
Who Are You?
Focus on the Right Things

Who is she?

You want to do something great for yourself and others, but you're afraid of making mistakes. You fear failure. You're not confident enough to do the right things. Instead, you focus too much on doing the things right.

You want to become a great woman, but you're afraid of the criticism. You fear rejection. You're not confident enough to express yourself in your own way. Instead, you focus on being like the others.

You want to start your own business, but you're afraid of failing. You also fear the success that you can't handle. You're not confident enough to tell the world that you have a brilliant idea. Instead, you focus on negative thoughts.

You want to become the leader, but you're afraid of the norm. You fear rejection from people. You're not confident enough to prove them wrong. Instead, you focus on your flaws, and you try to prove them right by telling yourself that you're no good. No good in what? Only God can judge you, and you know that.

You want to make your parents proud, but you're afraid of the high standard. You fear your parents' rules. You're not confident enough to change anything, nor do you want to set a higher standard for yourself and your family. Instead, you focus on the same problems that have been haunting you and your family for years.

You want to study harder, but you're afraid of hard work. You fear the mistakes which might or might not happen. You're not confident enough to learn more or practice outside the class. Instead, you focus on the comparison with your classmates. You think they're short, but their score is always high. Wait, what?

You want to be a voice in your family, but you're afraid of problems. You fear the conflict. You're not confident enough to stop the problem from happening.

You want to be who you are, but you're afraid of yourself. You fear the failure brought by your own action or idea.

Failure is not a sign of weakness, but it's proof that you're creative enough to live and to do something different from yesterday.

You may say, "*But, Author, I fail every day. Every single day. What do you say?*"

It's the proof of your creativity. You don't want to live in your comfort zone, do you? You want to make a difference, right?

Regardless of whatever problem that might happen, you can always do the best you could in order to improve your life because your life is the choice that you make, not an obligation that you owe to anybody. You may fail along the way, but that's okay as long as you do the right things. Soon enough, you'll succeed. **Focus on the right things**, and nothing else!

Your life is a choice, not an obligation. It's your choice, not somebody else's order. It's always about your creativity, not your failure. Your life is about you, not others.

In short, your life is about who you are.

But who are you?

WHO IS SHE

20
Choose to Be
Who You Are

Who are you?

First of all, your school doesn't define who you are. What you study is just a small fraction of your life. What you work is another part of your life. At home, you may find a different version of yourself. Somewhere along the way, you will learn about who you really are. Sometimes you could have some clues about who you are.

> You question yourself, usually unfavorably. *"Why am I so stupid?"*

"Why can't I be smart like others?"
"Why am I so tall and pretty?"
Okay, maybe you never ask that last question!

Girl, you can choose to be who you are. You don't need to choose to be like the others. Truth be told that we all are different. I agree with that. If you expect to experience the same thing like others, you'll be wasting your time.

Personally, many girls whom I know are good, but all girls are different. I get along well with them because they never do any harmful things to me. They respect me the way I am. They never judge me for being weird. Simply, they just accept who I am.

For me, who I am is what I choose to be. I don't let my mom tell me about who I really am. I never allow my formal education to brag about my small achievement. I don't even care about my degree because I learn that my degree can do little to nothing if I don't do anything useful for society.

We all are different. You don't have to be like your cousin, anyway. You don't need to act too girly if you don't want to. As long as you don't hurt anybody, you can choose to live to be who you are. Society doesn't punish honest people, but those who are half-honest will pay the price for their own choice. I take myself as an example.

Who is the real Dara Ly?

In fact, he is just an introvert. He loves darkness. He loves being alone, and he loves peace. He loves being unpredictable, and he loves to be creative. The funny part is that he loves to be misunderstood or misjudged, in some ways. He loves to be unique, in short.

What he loves is what he wants to create for himself, but what he learns is what he has to follow in order to please others. You see? If he focuses on what he loves, then his life is all about what he creates or invents.

Ironically, if he has to focus on what he learns from others, then his life would be all about doing things right and follow the old path from the old generations.

Now ask yourself: "*Do I have to be like the rest?*" Have you found the right answer yet? I bet you have.

You need to choose the answer by yourself and for yourself. Choose to be anything you like as long as you don't hurt anybody. Choose to be who you are.

Let me ask you again: "Who are you?"

WHO IS SHE

Part 3
Her Personal Rules
Her Ways of Life!

DARA LY

21
Her Roles
Busy

Who is she?

She has played so many roles that she could hardly define who she is. Her life, however, is understood in one word: BUSY!

Busyness is what she has always known her entire life. She's raised by a family whose value is hard work, so it is common for her to work from dawn to dusk each day. Every day she has to help her mom with housework before going to school. Sometimes she skips breakfast as her class starts just about ten minutes after she finishes the housework. Luckily, the school is nearby.

She believes that she can do more than what is expected of her, so she trains herself to handle as many tasks as possible, and she never complains about her busyness. At least, not to her mother. This thoughtful daughter looks up to her mother and appreciates what her mother has done for her and the family.

If life at home is a busy life, high school would be a super busy life for her. A girl with great ambition like her is willing and able to pay a great price just to get what she aims for. Education is a part of her life, as she has been taught at home and school. Automatically, she expects herself to be busier than she could be. It means that no matter how busy she is, she could always do a few more tasks and complete a few more lessons, every day. She believes in hard work, so she gives herself many difficult tasks to complete each day. It's amazing how she could survive this far, by the way.

WHO IS SHE

After graduating from high school, she expects to be less busy. Her expectation fails her, for this time. During high school years, she was not concerned about what subjects she had to study, nor did she dislike busyness. However, university life has offered different ways to look at these common things.

In high school, it is common to take as many as eight subjects a year. Not to mention language classes both full time and part time. University life has redefined the definition of the word "common." That's how she feels about university. Nothing is common. Everything is new and unexpected.

Instead of taking many extra classes, she is required to complete many assignments. She thought she could finally stop worrying about semester exams from the 12th grade. She's wrong; she has to sleep in fear almost every night, worrying about the surprise quiz. Her fear is not without ground, by the way. A surprise quiz comes faster than a surprise birthday, given the fact that her birthday only comes once every four years!

Nevertheless, the challenge from university life is made harder because of the major she has to study also. Although she is naturally good at math, she is less enthusiastic about any major that involves a math subject. As hard as it sounds, accounting is what she is asked to choose.

She doesn't like it that much, but she could go along to get along with this new challenge. To her, it's just a challenge, and she is prepared to overcome these four years of education in order to pursue something that she likes. What does she like? She wants to start her own business.

DARA LY

She is yet to find out the advantage of accounting once she has a business of her own. For the time being, accounting is anything but an advantage. In fact, it's a pain in the neck. Everything is boring and unlikable. She doesn't like it that much. Well, not enough to invest her time to excel at it. As a result, she's a so-so student in her class.

What she learns from this lesson is very simple. If you let your parents tell you what to study but you do not like it, you will disappoint them because you are more likely to fail to do your best. Instead, you just do what you are told in order to survive from one semester to the next. That is not the best way to pursue higher education. That's more like pressure.

From Tony the Cat

Kitties and gentle-meows, let me tell you about busyness. There are two types of busyness: Busy & Lazy.

You are either busy with what you love to do, or you are lazy to do what you hate to do. It's good, and it's bad too. Why?

Believe me, sometimes what you see can deceive you of the truth. For example, when a cat sleeps from 6 AM till 8 PM, he (the cat) is busy. It looks like laziness, to you, maybe. But to the cat, it's his duty to sleep during the day time, in order to gain energy for night hunting. How am I so sure? Been there, done that.

My point is very simple. You either choose what you love to do, or your life will suffer from what you hate. You don't have to take my word for it, anyway.

There are times when people hate what they used to love. Sometimes they even hate whom they used to love. It's fair to say that you should read the next chapter to find out more about the woman.

Who is she?

22
Her Policy
The Best

Who is she?

She's a high school kid whose goal is to be the best! She wants to be the best in what she is doing. Her job as a student is to learn what she could as well as what she is being taught.

It does sound simple, but it is not always easy to reach this goal. Limitation is the barrier to her goal. She knows that she still allows *the small mind* to dominate her mind.

Generally, *the small mind* is the self-limited belief that has been misinterpreted by many people. *The small mind* is the limitation being placed upon us. The opposite of *the small mind* is **the smart mind**.

The smart mind is the genius that lives inside each and every one of us. That's right, only a fool would view everything based only on the size. The genius views it differently. God makes a genius out of us, but we make a fool out of ourselves. Self-limited belief is the making of the fool, and one should control it if she wants to be the genius.

She views her mind based on *the small mind* versus **the smart mind**. It sounds pretty strange to others, but not to her. By nature, she knows that she is a smart kid. That's why she aims at being the best. Be that as it may, she is aware of *the small mind* and how it could invade her belief system. That's why she is careful about what she thinks or says.

Her message to others is: **Use the smart mind, and leave the small mind alone.**

WHO IS SHE

23
Her Life
Odd

Who is she?

She is a high school student, but, very soon, she is going to graduate, and she will continue to the next level in university. She just needs to complete one last thing: *The national exam*!

As a kid, she was told that everybody was ordinary, and that also included her. That's how she behaved, or, at least, learned to blend in. She learned to be ordinary and to be just like everyone else. However, deep down, she knew she was anything but ordinary.

As she grows up, she starts to see the dots, and she begins to connect them in a pattern that only she could understand. In other words, she designs a different path for her life. It's the kind of life that seems odd to the rest of her friends, and unknown to many. Although she's

been told to follow the crowd, it is clear in her mind that she would always choose to be herself, no matter what.

It is easy to choose conformity and to listen without questioning, but she is a weird girl because she doesn't like listening to other people without having to debate with them. Or at least, she's debating inside her head. One can only imagine what it's like to have two options in everything she does. She always has two options.

Usually, she would decide to do something based on what she loves, and she would avoid anything that she hates. For example, talking to people is what she hates, so she avoids small talk. Especially with the elder people. It's not that she hates people. She doesn't hate anybody, but she just doesn't like talking too much.

There are a few exceptions, however, for the people she likes. Even though she's a solo-kind-of person, there are chances when she makes friends with the same type of people.

Who is she?

(**Author**: Who knows?)

WHO IS SHE

24
Her Privacy
Careful

Who is she?

She's so secretive that nobody could understand her way of life. On the surface, she appears shy and humble because she doesn't want to reveal her true nature. One reason is obvious; the society she lives in doesn't always celebrate the differences. She understands that part of the deal, so she chooses not to express much unless she has to.

On social media, she barely shows any information about herself. Privacy is her top priority, so she doesn't want anyone to know more than they have to. Rarely has she posted any pictures of herself. It's not because she's ugly. In fact, she's pretty.

Well, she just doesn't like posting pictures. Maybe she doesn't know how to use the filter? Or maybe she just doesn't care much about social media. The latter is more likely to be true.

Her privacy on social media is as important as her private life. Many kids may not know it, but many phone applications actually could use their information for some purposes which are not helpful at all. Luckily, she has understood the importance of keeping her privacy on social media in check. She only allows certain types of information that are required by the social media community guidelines.

Sometimes her friends would tell her that she's too careful. To her, it's just a way she lives her life. By that, it means a careful way of living.

DARA LY

She believes that the information on social media can be a double-edge sword, so she has to be careful with what to show and what to keep to herself.

Who is she?

WHO IS SHE

25
Her Dream
How to Succeed

Who is she?

She's a girl with many dreams. Her age doesn't limit her ability to dream and to imagine her future. This girl wants to travel to places. She wants to be independent and to be successful. To many people, it's just a dream, but to her, it's the future she must have, so she chooses to walk toward it.

She dares to dream big because she is able to do so, with the help of self-knowledge and courage. She doesn't look at herself and sees weakness. In contrast, she sees herself as the champion. She views her life as a gift from God, and she knows everything will be good for her if she chooses to follow her heart and work hard to reach her goal(s) in the future. How to succeed in her dream is entirely up to her because she's the boss.

A big dream requires a strong commitment, and a true vision demands a true passion to fulfill it. She's got the dream, and she's got the plan. Most importantly, she believes in herself. Anybody who has a clear purpose for something will be able to achieve it, one way or another. She understands that concept very well because she lives it each and every day. She focuses on a few things in her life because there are not many things that she has to worry about. She never has to worry about what people have to say about her since she gets used to being alone.

For most people, loneliness is the worst nightmare, but to her, it is an inspirational friend. Being alone gives her enough time to think. It teaches her to be stronger too. She used to feel weak, but loneliness had forced the weakness to abandon her since the day she decided to become a strong woman who can live alone as long as she so desires.

She has redefined the definition of loneliness, and she makes it her friend, a friend who is rather helpful than harmful. It wasn't easy in the beginning, however. She had to deal with the same experience when she was left alone by the people she loved. Instead of blaming them for leaving her, she chose to learn from this hurtful experience and learn to live with it.

Who is she?

WHO IS SHE

26
Her Standard
High

Who is she?

She's a woman with a high standard for herself and a strong will to get what she wants. Even though her way of life might have been predetermined by her parents as she was younger, they allow her to choose what she wants for her future. Especially, what she wants to study. She chooses her major in medical school, which is more challenging than anything else that she likes. Needless to say, she has a will so strong that nothing could stand in her way, and she expects to achieve her goal.

A high standard is her rule, but the rules from the schools where she attends still give her a lot of pressure. Generally speaking, everybody is expected to perform well, and that also includes her. She has to try more than she could ever imagine. It's like chasing after perfection.

Sometimes she also doubts herself. She's wondering if she's putting too much pressure on herself, or she's way behind her classmates. But who is she?

There's a common joke among her friends. They say something like: "*Don't try too hard, or you'll get old and look like a ghost soon.*"

A woman whose standard of life is high usually has a personal issue with beauty as well. It does make sense, though. She is naturally pretty, but that's not enough to keep her happy. She often complains that her look is not acceptable.

The thing is, it's her insecurity issue that causes the trouble. That's why she covers her look with a filter whenever she takes a selfie.

She would say: "*Author, that's a normal thing to use a filter. Don't you use it too?*"

She's right. I also use it, but not too much. In fact, it's okay to use a filter as long as it's not too much. We can say the same thing about a high standard. It's good to have a high standard and stick to it, but it's not advisable to put too much pressure on yourself. Now I sound like an old fart again. I mean, who in the world wouldn't put pressure in order to be the best they can be? Right?

That's what I thought too. Dara Ly used to be super disciplined and strict on himself, but he didn't like himself at all, regardless of what he had achieved. He gave up all parts of himself just for work, and ignored the rest of the world. Simply, he couldn't care less about anything or anybody. That also included the family and loved ones.

Now enough about me. You need to make your own conclusion about your life and the way you want to live it. If you have a high standard, it'll be good. Keep in mind that a high standard is also a form of pressure. When your will is strong, it'll be great. A strong will is a form of commitment.

When you can balance between your commitment and pressure, your life will be better. Not a lot of people can do that, though. But you're still young, meaning that you can retry and retry. Right?

WHO IS SHE

27
Her Message
Be Beautiful and Be Smart

Who is she?

She is a beautiful woman, with or without makeup. Okay, that sounds too simple.

What else can I say? I mean, that's the truth about her. Believe me, she's really beautiful. And smart! Don't forget that part!

Some people say that pretty girls ain't smart, but I have a completely different view. Most beautiful girls I've met are sharp. In other words, they ain't dumb like some dumbos have said. It's a dumb idea to conclude that way.

She is a beautiful and smart woman, but she can't be happy because her surrounding environment is not supportive enough. Some people quickly judge on her dress, and, needless to say, they say bad things about her.

Yeah, this kind of thing still exists nowadays. The only problem is that she can't find peace with herself when she hears from them. It's just too annoying!

Sometimes she wonders whether she should accept their judgment or reject it. Still, it ain't a pretty feeling to hear that. She decides to avoid them, but she also avoids people in general. As a result, she learns to dislike people fast.

More or less, she tends to be isolated from people. Outwardly, she appears to be shy. People take that as a form of stupidity or weakness. That's when they are wrong about her. This woman sees all and hears all. She ain't stupid nor weak.

Who is she?

In short, society may see her in the wrong way, and that's okay because she never views herself that way. Deep down, she knows she's a strong woman, and she's smart. She's also beautiful.

The message she wants to send to other women is very simple. Her message is: **Be beautiful, and be smart. More importantly, be yourself.**

WHO IS SHE

28
Her Suggestion
The Obstacle

Who is she?

Her Suggestion:

You could be smart, and still something could stand in your way. What are you going to do with that? Are you going to let the obstacle ruin your life? Or will you fight back?

It's time to decide. Be firm in your decision, and be bold in your action. A wishy-washy action won't work. You need to evaluate your effort in living your life.

A support system is also what you need when you set out to make your life a happy story. To walk a long way, you'll need motivating factors. To succeed in your life, you'll need people who care for you and can comfort you when you fail. Everybody fails, and that's okay. It's better than doing nothing.

Like the Italian proverb goes: "He who does nothing does not fail."

The key point is that you don't quit, in good times and bad. Take charge of your life, and aim for your success. When you face an obstacle, overcome it. When you fall down, get up. When you fall down again, get up again.

DARA LY

Then you ask: "What if I fall asleep?"

Well, just don't forget to set an alarm clock before you fall asleep. Okay?

Now you ask again: "But who is she, Author?"

(*Dara Ly is sleeping...*)

WHO IS SHE

29
He Is Shoe...
He Is What?

Who is she?

He is shoe...

He is what?

Truth be told that this book is written in order to empower young women, so basically, all messages should be about women. However, this one is an exception; it will be about a man.

But who is he?

Well, he's a shoe-less boy who has become a servant of God. It sounds weird, but it's true. Today, he is ready to declare the true purpose of his life because he doesn't want to remain untrue to himself and The Big Boss up there.

Who is he?

(Let's talk about something else?)

One lesson I've learned from my own setback is to look and see what I will be seeing in the next five years. It's motivating me to work hard to realize such a goal. Now it's become my second nature to see what I will be seeing in the distant future, as if it's right here in front of me. It's refreshing because I can be sure that I won't quit, no matter how tough my life has been or could be.

It's not a delusion, but you have to be certain. Never doubt your decision. Anyone who doubts herself will always be unsure of what she could or should do. That's the lesson I've learned. When in doubt, I remind myself about one simple truth. **I come here to serve humanity.** That's all I need to know. Before knowing that, I always had one question for myself.

I asked myself: "*Why would I want to serve others?*"

I mean, let's face it, people suffer all the time. Every day, people die. You see problems everywhere you go. With or without my service, people still suffer.

Why do I have to try to change things? That's the question I kept asking myself. In other words, I wasn't sure why I should do what I can do.

Then I realized that simple truth: "**I come here to serve humanity.**"

Now I fully embrace my work and won't try to hide it anymore. Don't get me wrong. I'm not trying to do anything sinister. My work is simple; I am here to serve humanity. I'm sure I'll make some mistakes along the way. Those could be unintentional also, but, with the help of The Big Boss up there, I'll be able to get things done, and done right.

I just need to start now. One step at a time!

When my mission is accomplished, I'll go back to meet My Maker. It's a long way back home, I guess!

WHO IS SHE

30
Her Fear
Her Family

Who is she?

She wants to be an independent woman, and she has a dream. Her dream is to travel the world by herself. She might be a little girl, for now, but she has a heart big enough to conquer her fear and the limitations placed by her family. This little girl has her own ideas about how to live a happy life, but her ideas clash with many things that surround her. She wishes to have more freedom to choose, but she knows she's under the control of her parents. It means she has to be patient. She also needs to prove to her parents that she is strong now and able to choose for herself.

But who is she?

More often than not, she questions the things that her parents tell her. She's a little confused, not knowing

what to do. By nature, she is a free spirit, so her free will often clashes with the will of her parents. They want her to listen and follow them, but she always has questions in her head. She doesn't want to admit that her parents are wrong, but she knows she is doing the right thing. That's the conflict in her mind right now.

Why is that? The reason is obvious; as a conformist, a woman is taught to behave and to be obedient, no matter what. It's like the water. If you keep it in the glass, it stays in the glass. If it is in the river, it flows to many places. A woman is like the water, in a sense of flexibility and wisdom. Yet, her options could be limited by a lot of factors, such as family, society, norm, and so on.

DARA LY

Should we give a woman her freedom and her rights to choose? I wholeheartedly agree.

But it's not my position to make the call. She has to make the decision by herself. It's the decision that would impact her life.

To be free or to be helpless?

You need to choose by yourself and for yourself.

WHO IS SHE

**PART 4
BECAUSE SHE CAN**
It's Time to Shine!

31
Be Happy
You Can

Who is she?

I don't want to sound too biased, but I just want to speak for my little sister who has to deal with heartache alone after she broke up with a guy who left her nothing but a scar. I can't tell you what kind of scar.

If you love yourself enough, you will understand the meaning of life. When someone leaves you, you will have to make up your own mind. Wait for him or let his pictures be removed from your memory store. I know, sometimes you cannot remove them easily, but at least, you can hide them, can't you? You can and you should. Believe me, you can forget those bad things and move on. How?

I suggest you meet people with the same heartache experiences. **Talk to them. Listen to their stories.** Don't try to make any judgment. Put yourself into the same situations, and you will see the whole picture. You will find out what's going on. It can help you recover from your pain. Maybe you can help them too when you listen to them.

If you want to make a bigger positive impact, then I suggest **you start writing** to inform and inspire others who have faced similar problems. It will help them heal faster, and it could help you forget those things as well. I write when I am unhappy. It helps me learn a lot of things that I neglected before. Writing opens my heart once again. It keeps me honest with myself. When you are honest with yourself, things will get better and better.

WHO IS SHE

If writing is not a good solution for you, then I have another suggestion: **Reading!**

The good news is that you are doing just that. You are reading Dara Ly's book right now. I can guarantee that you will fall asleep soon. I'm just kidding.

Reading helps you think. It also allows you to relax because it requires a good mood and good environment. When you have a good reading habit, your life might as well improve. Why? Because reading is a sleeping pill. I got you again.

Reading is really helpful, and it can cure your pain and solve many puzzling issues in the past. When you

are reading, you will review a lot of old memories from the past. Some are good.

Oh, you remember the time you were playing with your childhood friends and your mom was searching for you everywhere. You were nowhere to be found because your friends found you before your mother did; they gave a signal that your mama was running around with a small stick, shouting for your name, so loud like a megaphone. Do you remember that one?

Now you remember the time after school when you rushed quickly to watch the TV at the neighbor's house. Do you remember that one?

If reading cannot help you much, I suggest you take a vacation. **Maybe traveling should help.** Oh, you're saying that it's impossible because you have to work?

Then I have yet another solution. **Work.** One more solution is work. Yes, work, work, work! Keep yourself busy. Many people keep themselves busy in order to forget their heartbreak moments. This method works even if it does hurt at the same time. I remember when I was very depressed and feeling useless. I gave myself so many projects to complete. I kept myself busy day and night.

Keeping yourself busy might be a good solution. But what if you are too lazy to do all those things? Then there

is another unhealthy solution that you should avoid. Yes, you should avoid it. Please avoid dramatic stories on social media.

If you see the Newsfeed, chances are you would feel sorry for yourself for many reasons. Luckily, I never checked the Newsfeed, so I had no idea if my friends were getting married or getting divorced. Whatsoever! It's like I was living on an island. You know?

If you can't get away from Facebook, then I suggest you use it for good. Maybe you can chat to some old friends and ask them about their lives. Somehow it can help you feel relieved after hearing random stories from people you care for. One of my friends used to tell me that when she was really sad, she would talk to other sad people. When she heard about their stories, she started to feel motivated. She learned that she should be thankful for not having to face worse problems that others had to deal with.

Be happy!
Because you can!

WHO IS SHE

32
Be Alone
It's Okay

Who is she?

She is free, and she can do anything she wants. She doesn't have to answer to anybody. This lonely world is preparing her to become a real woman. She will know that she is no longer a little girl, so some things have to change. She has to change the ways she views this world. Lonely world simply means a free-will zone for her to play. She can play, and she doesn't have to worry because this place is harmless for her.

Isn't it a good thing to be alone? She will taste the real joy of freedom and how to spend it without having to worry about tomorrow. Your freedom is unlike money. You can spend your freedom as you please, but you can't spend money like a boss if you are still asking for your mom's money. If she gives you the kind of freedom you want, I promise you it will be unlimited. The more you spend it, the better you feel.

Who is lucky enough to have this kind of freedom? Guess who? The lonely girl. A girl who is alone can eventually find herself in the middle of joy and misery. If she chooses joy, the lonely world would simply mean freedom. If she chooses misery, it would mean darkness.

This world has ruined her life. Who can help her? She can help herself, but she needs to change the way she solves a problem. Agree?

How to change? She should change the way she thinks. She should change the way she speaks. She can change the way she dresses if she wants. She can change the way she views the world.

DARA LY

She doesn't like to be left alone, but she hates being surrounded by people, so she learns to be solo. She is a brilliant artist, in her own view, and she never stops finding out about the beauty in it as she has devoted her time to perfect her art.

People who are left alone are the ones who come out stronger and better, in so many ways. Most of us would be very surprised to see the same person with a different image (personality). One of the positive things about this is that she has grown to be a mature woman.

These solo people are those that make great things possible in the history of mankind. Albert Einstein is a brilliant example, if we talk about a lonely yet brilliant mind.

She doesn't want to feel isolated from the class, but she hates to join crazy talk, or even normal conversation with her classmates. In turn, nobody would want to talk to her, either. It's fair enough, isn't it?

She feels insecure when she is with other people, so she prefers to be forgotten by those who don't matter in her daily life. Yet her parents never forget to remind her that she should behave like a normal girl. Well, guess what, in her mind, she believes she will feel abnormal when she tries to blend into the crowd of people. She just wants to stay away. In other words, she only wants to stay at home because she's a home lover.

Now you think to yourself, "*He is talking about me. Oh my God! I'm so embarrassed.*"

But please let me reassure you, there's nothing to be ashamed of, my amazing *Team Solo*. I'm one of you, and I am proud to say that we all are amazing and brilliant when we are alone because it is when we truly focus on our thoughts and select only the best of them.

WHO IS SHE

I will say this: **Home lovers are amazing people.**

Why? Because your parents should be glad when you're home all the time.

You'll say, "*Wrong! My parents always blame me.*" Blame for what? For the fact that you sleep at home, doing nothing for the rest of the day? Yeah, I can relate to that, but, believe me, they will never have to worry about you because they know you are safe at home. One thing they will never ever find out is...

What is that? You want to know about it? Good, let me skip it then. Okay, okay, I'll tell you later. Now let me talk about her a little more. I mean, YOU!

She blames her introverted personality and feels very upset about it. Of course, she has every reason to be sad because she often kicks people out of her life even if she wants them to stay, at least, for a while. Why does she do that? Why kick them out if you want them to be with you?

She'll say: "*Because I'm a bad person.*"

I hope she didn't say that. Unfortunately, she used to think like that. If she is reading it right now, here is my message to her: "*You're not that bad!*"

It's okay to be alone as long as you're happy. You can be alone and happy!

33
Be Everything
She Chooses to Be

Who is she? She chooses to be everything she wants to be because she can. These are a few things about her:

- She thinks she is a weird person.
- She doesn't like to go to a crowded place.
- She expresses her feelings so well.
- God created her to show others how to be selfless, and that's exactly who she is. She always thinks about others before herself, hardly doing anything for herself.
- She believes that finding someone's happiness is her own happiness.
- She takes people's relationships seriously, and she puts herself in their shoes.
- She is a woman with compassion, sympathy, care, and understanding.
- She tries to understand others' feelings and refuses to let them down. She always tries to help them without expecting anything in return.
- She is an emotional girl, so to speak. Even a simple thing can cause her tremendous stress. Usually, this woman overthinks and every night abuses herself with tears and misery. She needs the right person to show her that she can love and be loved once again.

- She needs someone she can talk to. Someone who does not judge her stories. Someone who will always

WHO IS SHE

tell her that she has the most beautiful stories to tell the world. Someone who will never get bored of listening to her. Someone who will always remember and remind her about her own greatness as a woman. Someone who can correct her just in time of need. Someone who will stay by her side no matter what happens. Someone who will protect her heart. Someone who will never ever give up on her. Someone who is loyal to her, under any circumstances. Someone who loves her for no reason. Someone who cares for her. Someone who can lend her his shoulder. Someone who will talk and share the shadow with her until they both get old. Someone who will hold her hand forever and won't let go. Someone who knows she is not perfect but still refuses to love another girl. Someone who will make her life beautiful every day. Someone who will do anything he could to be with her. Someone who loves her parents the same way she does. Someone who treats her friends with respect and understanding. She just needs someone like that.

- She is an emotional person, but inside this fragile emotion lives a beautiful soul that is full of love.
- She loves an adventurous lifestyle and wants to go to many places. She has always dreamed of a solo trip, and she has always been fond of traveling to any place that could reenergize her soul. Exotic country, perhaps. Or maybe somewhere in this beautiful country. She wants to learn something new and useful because she knows life will provide many things as a form of lesson. She alone will have to learn and absorb

the knowledge. Of course, her parents do not seem to be fond of all these things. Let alone a solo adventure to a faraway place from home. To them, this idea is very dangerous. They love her too much to let her do that. However, this woman has the spirit of a bird. Free like a bird, flies high like a plane, walks proudly on the planet Earth!

- She has always been independent since she was young because she knew early on that she would one day have to take care of her siblings and her parents. She has the obligation of a daughter and a sister also.
- After stepping her feet on the university soil, she knew she would be independent and had to be responsible for herself. Nobody was there to help her all the time. Thankfully, this was a strong-will woman with commitment to become an excellent student. She had exceeded her expectations. That didn't mean she had no obstacles. She had so many of them. There were countless problems, too many stressful assignments and a lot of things. Still, she could manage them all.
- She tried to survive from one semester to the next, but she never forgot her own discipline. She never asked anyone for help because she didn't think it was the right thing to do.
- She rides a motorbike alone, eats her meals alone, reads books alone, and of course, feels sleepy like a cat, alone also. Despite the fact that she has to ride far enough from home to school, she is also a home lover. If she doesn't need to deal with school work or a group assignment, she would prefer to sleep at home. You're

WHO IS SHE

right, SHE SLEEPS LIKE A LADY BOSS!

- She doesn't know what love really means. Some people say that she has no feeling. When it comes to love, she begins to feel like an alien. She is immune to this attachment feeling, so to speak. She rejects people who love her, and she waits for nobody. This is the kind of feeling every girl has when she is fed up with relationship problems. And it can occur time and time again. She doesn't even know what she is doing, by the way. She prefers to be a friend instead of a lover because she believes friendship lasts longer than the relationship.

- She believes that fate is created by us. Nobody can take away what belongs to us if we challenge ourselves to get it. She believes that we deserve to be the masters of life.
    - She doesn't love herself enough, and she doesn't want anyone to care about her because she is not a selfish person. It's hard for her to love herself.
    - Sometimes she ignores everything and enjoys life.
    - But she is like a kid because she sometimes cries for absolutely no reason. Every bad experience, bad thing or even a small problem can ruin her feelings.
    - She often feels lonely. Very lonely! Whenever she looks out, there is nobody to be found. Nobody is there to cheer her up.

- She's a stubborn girl. She doesn't accept anyone because she is afraid that she won't be given enough love and care from him. She usually knows before knowing it. It's known as the sixth sense or Scorpio sense.

WHO IS SHE

34

Be the Superwoman
Do You Know?

Who are you?

You have to believe in yourself. If you don't, you are not going to make it out successful and happy the way you want to be. You know that, don't you?

What else do you know?

At the workplace, things can turn rough or even worse, but you need to be calm because calmness is a cure for stress from work. Some people try to calm themselves by meditation. We don't forget those who have chosen the wrong way to calm themselves.

Those who drink too much beer. They believe it's how to calm themselves when they are not themselves. That's a miserable way to solve a problem. Of course, nobody wants to end up being miserable. You wouldn't want to even if you could. Would you? I'm glad that you said NO.

The suggestion is: **Say NO to beer!**

You're tired from work, and you have to sit in the class for three hours, and sleepy like hell. Nobody would bother you because it is your habit right now. Your job is not a big deal, and you seem to handle it just fine. On the contrary, your study has been affected dramatically. You don't have much time for a group assignment, and you hate the fact that you have to copy the homework from your friend.

It's okay to get lost in the middle of studying. Maybe you think your classmates are smarter than you. Maybe they could catch up a little faster than you. Maybe!

DARA LY

In the class, your classmates appear to be super smart. You have to work hard while they are resting. You have to run just to catch up with their walking speed. You have to fly if they are running. On top of that, they exceed your expectations, and that makes you upset because you feel left behind. The bad news is you are only half way from graduation. God knows how to make time go faster than usual, but it seems like your time in school is walking slowly like a turtle. What you hate the most about time is that it would always pass so fast if it is your holiday. "Time is unfair," you think. That's why you often say, "I don't have time."

From now on, you need to reverse your thoughts. The ways you think about your work and your study should be different. If you want a better result, you should have a better habit. Simple enough?

Anyway, you can choose to be who you want to be.

Choose the best version of yourself. What version?

To be the superwoman!

WHO IS SHE

35
Be Positive
Stay Positive

Who are you?

You are a positive person, you know that. But it seems like you are not being honest with yourself. Why did I say so? Because you think positively but act and speak otherwise. Remember the rules of peaceful life? You don't remember? Never mind, because I never told you. Not yet.

Here are the rules:

- Think positively
- Speak positively
- Act positively

If you have read my book "**Because I Was Selfish Volume 3,**" you would pick up another rule, in addition to these three simple rules.

What is it? "Stay single!"

I'm kidding. The rule invented by the **Machine** is "Stay positive." Now we have four rules:

- Think positively
- Speak positively
- Act positively
- Stay positive (Stay single!)

You are a woman easily touched by emotional stuff. Even a small thing that people take for granted can hurt your feelings. Sometimes you wonder why you don't like someone without a reason, even if that person doesn't have anything to do with you and your peace of mind. You are an emotional kid with a two-in-one mindset. We're talking about the positive mindset and negative mindset. It's my obligation to bring back your positive mindset and put it in place because I know you will do a lot of great things in the future.

I know you are a woman of great potential and you are strong from the inside. You are a beautiful soul with a beautiful life, but you need to be positive. I mean, you should follow the three simple rules of life.

Let me repeat them again: **Think positive thoughts. Speak positive words. Act positive actions.**

Your life has transformed dramatically. Have you noticed that? From a carefree girl to a superwoman. From a countryside girl to a respectful and cultivated woman whom everybody admires. From an immature (I'd like to use your own word) to a sophisticated woman in the modern time. From a clueless mind to a powerful mind. There are many other life-transforming points that you have experienced and you understand that life is about changing one form to another. The truth is beautiful things can always happen if you are positive about life.

I hope, in this book, it also feels like we are talking like we always do, on Facebook. I do hope you find it refreshing and energizing. I hope you can release stress after reading this book.

Be positive!

Do we have a deal?

36
Be Strong
No Need

Who are you?

No crying. No self-pity. No need for the blame game. All you need is yourself. All you need to know is that you are strong. Stronger than you thought you could be. The universe has a way to create coincidence and prove that you are not the product of mediocrity. You are the most qualified person to become the ruler of the united beings (yourself). When your heart and your mind unite as one, nothing can break you. Nothing can stand in your way. You are strong. You are powerful. You are the superwoman!

Don't pretend that you can lose in the game of life. You will never ever lose anything in this game because you have nothing to lose.

The real strength comes from belief. Be strong!

37

Be the Best
When You Were Young

Who are you?

Imagine when you were young and the fun things that you enjoyed doing. The moment you realize that it has gone is the moment you know you need to grow up and move on to living a new type of life. It is similar to the life you had in high school. You had enjoyed many things which left a smile on your face.

One day you look back, and you might realize that everything that happened before is forever a memory because you need not go back to retake the exam that once scared you. You realize that your math teacher was right. He predicted that you would become a respectful person. You did become like one.

People respect you because you are a good person. You don't have to be the most beautiful girl. Well, I'm not saying you should be the ugliest, either. You don't have to be the greatest kid in the world. Of course, not the worst kid, either. You don't have to be the smartest person on the planet, but you have to do and be the best you can. Always do the right thing.

Be yourself, and be the best you can be.

WHO IS SHE

38
Be Cool
Worry Is Not Healthy

Who are you?

You are a fine woman, but you need to watch the way you view everything around you. People have no intention to hurt your feelings, so you might as well leave them alone and mind your own business. We have seen many people who have trouble sleeping at night because they are too busy blaming a lot of things, which in fact, have nothing to do with them.

You cannot free yourself when you are worrying. Worry is not healthy; it only exploits your productive mind. I suggest you stop worrying. Stop worrying over small things, and start to free yourself. You could and you should enjoy your life, instead of stressing out. Don't you agree?

You can go to the next level if you are willing to listen and learn what you can. Stop pretending that you know everything. Only a fool could do that. You are a genius. A genius knows when to ask the right question. She knows that a problem can occur, and her job is not to avoid a problem but to fix it. If understanding is one of your problems, then I suggest you start listening to others from now on. Can you do that? You can do that. I know you can.

If your problem is about study, why don't you start learning from now on? Can you do that? You can do that. I know you can. But wait a minute, if it had been that easy, you would have done that a long time ago, right? That's right. It ain't easy all the time.

I suggest you spend some time alone in order to focus on your study. You see, the exam is coming, so the clock is ticking.

DARA LY

Stop wasting your time, and start asking your friends if you can join them in study group. Join as many groups as possible. Be committed, and stick with the groups. You can do it.

I know you will experience new feelings. I've been there, and done that. I joined as many study groups as possible only to make sure my crush would be interested in me. It worked; she fell in love with my best friend. Yes. Didn't I say that you should join as many study groups as possible? You got it; my best friend was also there with me even if he was not that active like Dara Ly the nerd. He was smart by nature, but I was nothing like him, and that's how I had to study the whole night till 4 AM, while he would be drinking coffee or eating noodles with some other boys. God, I was so jealous.

My point is simple. Work hard, and focus on the good things even though sometimes your luck isn't that good.

Someday it will improve, and you shall find a good person. I have found more than one! And they're better than good, I should say.

Work hard, and focus on yourself. Find the ways to improve yourself and your life. Aim at improving what you are doing.

Don't worry! Be cool! Be yourself!

WHO IS SHE

39
Be True
To Yourself

Who are you?

Let me tell you a story about a girl whose dream is to become an architect. What a beautiful dream she's got. Don't you agree? Unfortunately, this dream is torn apart before it comes into form. By whom? Her mom.

She told me that her mom wants her to become a school teacher. That's her mom's dream. Actually, becoming a school teacher is a good thing because a teaching career is a prestigious job, and being a teacher is great. But she has her heart set on being an architect. *"Sorry, mom, but I want to live my own dream by my own right. But I will make you proud, mom."*

There is another story about my friend who has been through countless life lessons. A girl who refuses to cry even if she should be sorry for herself. Well, she refuses to cry. She learns how to smile while trying to hide those sad stories and unforgettable memories left by her very own father.

There's another untold story from an unknown girl who calls herself Queen of Drama. Before we get into her dramatic things, here is what we should learn from this little girl. Apparently, she's a little short, shorter than her friends, so to speak. Perhaps the shortest of all, her friends would say. Please don't tell her about that, or she'll throw my book away for sure. Oh, and, please don't tell her that I adore her very much just like the soup needs the salt. When talking about soup, I begin to get hungry again.

By the way, she's a little girl with a big dream. She's hungry for happiness. She is willing to invest her time for education.

Why? Because she wants to be a good daughter for her mom and for her dad also.

Now are you ready to hear about her drama? Good. Then let me tell you about another girl who shares the same nickname, Queen of Drama. Actually, they both are like drama twins. They have shared many things in common.

The point is you should be true to yourself. Life can be tough from time to time, but nothing should change your nature. Your nature is honesty. I'm not saying it's easy to be who you are and remain honest, but it's easier than disappointment. Don't you agree?

Nothing is more disappointing than to fake yourself just to be accepted. Been there, done that! It ain't pretty!

The suggestion is: **Be true to yourself because you can.**

WHO IS SHE

40
Be Different
So Be It

Who am I?

They said that I was rude. Well, I was not rude, but I was just being myself. The fact is, people don't like me because I am honest. They also love me because I am honest. In short, I can't please everyone, so I won't let anyone label me as anything I am not.

Of course, I won't need to try to stop them, for they'll never stop. But it doesn't make me the person they think I should be. I am who I am, and I am not trying to pretend to be somebody I am not.

I like boyish styles, and I hate girly things. So what?

I like working at night, and sleeping like a lady boss in the morning. So what?

I like Instagram better than Facebook. So what?

I don't like to chit chat pointlessly with strangers. So what? I don't like gossiping. So what?

People think that I am rude because I am not a tea-sugar type of girl like the ones they have known. If it is what they call rude, so be it. I'm not rude, anyway.

I am weird, and I know it, but I don't care as long as I am happy with myself. I also want you to know that everybody has his or her own way of life. You can't talk somebody into your own way of life just because you believe it is the only way everybody should follow. It just doesn't work for me.

I warn you not to intrude into my life, or we will no longer remain friends. If you like to be depressed, that's fine by me, but I am not going to copy the way you live. If you want to blame everything around you, that's fine by me, but I am not going to do the same, because I am not you.

I am different, and I am happy about that.

WHO IS SHE

Who is she?

Only she can define who she is!

Only God can judge her!

She answers to herself!

And herself only!

Don't miss out!

Visit the website below and you can sign up to receive emails whenever Dara Ly publishes a new book. There's no charge and no obligation.

https://books2read.com/r/B-A-HAXZ-FXGSC

BOOKS 2 READ

Connecting independent readers to independent writers.

Milton Keynes UK
Ingram Content Group UK Ltd.
UKHW010653080324
439098UK00001B/18